Enjoy Guided Reading!
Year 5

Teacher Book with Copymasters

Sarah St John

For the novels:

- *Charlotte's Web* by E.B. White
- *Goodnight Mister Tom* by Michelle Magorian
- *The Illustrated Mum* by Jacqueline Wilson
- *Seasons of Splendour* by Madhur Jaffrey
- *How the Whale Became and other stories* by Ted Hughes
- *The Snow Goose and other stories* by Paul Gallico

You may copy this book freely for use in your school.

The pages in this book are copyright, but copies may be made without fees or prior permission provided that these copies are used only by the institution which purchased the book. For copying in any other circumstances, prior written consent must be obtained from the publisher.

Badger Publishing

Introduction to Guided Reading

Criteria for selecting titles
The books are all fiction and include a range of popular titles, short stories and modern classics. They were selected after consultation with Advanced Skills Literacy teachers, Literacy co-ordinaters and Key Stage 2 class teachers. They contain a level of differentiation so that, for each year group, there are books that cover a range of abilities.

Titles
There are six titles for each year group. Each title has the following accompanying guidance:
- A chapter synopsis
- Text level reading objectives
- Notes for two guided reading sessions

Chapter synopsis
This section breaks the book down into chapters, thus familiarising teachers with unknown texts.

Text Level Reading objectives
Reading objectives for each title are taken from the National Literacy Strategy text level objectives and are specific to that particular year group. They are referred to throughout the two guided reading sessions and either form part of the group discussion or are targeted during the independent follow-up work.

Guided Reading Sessions
The two guided reading sessions are broken down as follows:

Guided reading session one
- Introduction to the text
- Strategy check
- Independent reading
- Return to text
- Two follow-up activities

Guided reading session two
- Response to the text
- Strategy check
- Independent reading
- Return to the text
- Two follow-up activities

Introduction to the text (session one only)
This section suggests ways in which the text can be introduced, for example through discussing the front cover and title, reading the blurb or the first part of the book prior to the first session and using this knowledge to discuss and make predictions on what the book is about, or what may happen.

Strategy check
In this section, reference is made to the following:

- Specific features of the text, for example the use of capital letters or exclamation marks to highlight the need for expression when reading.
- Developing reading strategies, such as the use of contextual clues to help decode unknown words within the text.
- Text level reading objectives and how they can be used to extend the children's understanding and enjoyment.

Independent reading
The children are given a reading focus and asked to read independently. For this part of the session, they will need either reading journals or whiteboards and pens so they can make notes related to the reading focus.

Return to the text
Follow-up questions are provided to facilitate discussion related to the independent reading task.

Follow-up activities
Two follow-up activities are suggested to support each guided reading session and, depending on the time available, just one or both the activities could be completed. Should there not be time to complete the follow-up activities in full, it is important that the children carry out the independent reading part of the activity so that they are prepared for the second guided reading session.

The follow-up activities involve interpreting the text in a range of ways, for example independently reading the text, making notes, writing mind maps, carrying out research or a more formal writing task. The writing tasks cover different forms of writing, for example letters, diary entries or newspaper reports, and are designed to add interest to the text. However, while there will not be time for the teacher to model the writing before the children begin the activity, the teacher may refer back to any previous class work completed in that style. It is important to note that, when marking the children's work, the emphasis should be placed on whether the children have interpreted the text correctly, rather than whether they are able to adopt the given style correctly.

Response to text (session two only)
This section contains questions specific to the follow-up activities at the end of session one and also general questions related to each of the chapters the children were required to read in preparation for the second guided reading session. While there may not be time to discuss all the chapters the children have read independently, teachers can choose to discuss one chapter in detail or select questions from each of the chapters.

Sarah St John

1 Charlotte's Web *by E.B. White*

Chapter Synopsis

Chapter 1 - Before Breakfast

Fern lives on a farm with her mum, dad and brother, Avery. One morning before breakfast, Fern's dad walks by with an axe. Her mum tells her that a litter of pigs has been born, but that one of them is a runt. Fern begs her father not to kill it, but he says that runts are trouble. In the end, her dad relents and says that she can look after it. Fern feeds the pig and, on the way to school, decides to name it Wilbur.

Chapter 2 - Wilbur

Fern loves Wilbur and looks after him well. He waits with her at the bus stop in the morning and follows her around after school. When Wilbur is five weeks old, her dad says she has to sell him as he's started to eat food and they can't afford to provide for him. Fern is distraught, but her mum suggests that they sell it to their neighbour, who also happens to be Fern's uncle. He buys it for six dollars and lets Fern visit whenever she wants to.

Chapter 3 - Escape

Wilbur's new home is a barn and, while Fern is allowed to sit and watch Wilbur, she is not allowed to take him out. Wilbur is pleased to have Fern there because he hasn't made friends with the other animals and is lonely and bored. When one of the geese sees Wilbur looking fed up, she tells him how he can escape. He escapes and goes off exploring, but Fern's aunt, Mrs Zuckerman, notices he's escaped and he is soon surrounded. The smell of slops that the farmer uses to tempt Wilbur back into the barn is finally too much and Wilbur is captured. The loose board is nailed into place and Wilbur thinks he is too young for the world.

Chapter 4 - Loneliness

Wilbur wakes up and finds it's raining which spoils his plans for the day. He asks the other animals to play with him, but they are either too busy or not interested. Wilbur becomes very depressed and the farmer notices and gives him some medicine. Later on that night, Wilbur hears a voice in the darkness asking if he wants a friend. The voice says she's been watching him all day and likes him. She tells Wilbur they will meet in the morning.

Chapter 5 - Charlotte

Wilbur can't sleep. Not only do the noises in the barn keep him awake, but he is also excited at the prospect of having a friend. When he wakes up, he asks around to see who his new friend is, but no one speaks up. The sheep tells him that the animal is probably still asleep. Later on, the new friend calls to Wilbur. She is a spider called Charlotte, but Wilbur is worried that he can't like her because he doesn't like the bloodthirsty way she kills her prey. However, Charlotte will prove herself to be a loyal friend.

1

Chapter 6 - Summer Days

Once school ends, Fern is at the farm everyday. She spends time with Wilbur and she and Avery also help out with the haymaking. The goose's eggs hatch and there are seven goslings, but one of the eggs doesn't hatch and Templeton, the rat, wants it. The gander gives it to him, but warns him against going near the goslings.

Chapter 7 – Bad News

Wilbur grows to like Charlotte, but one of the sheep upsets him by saying that the farmer is only fattening him up so he can kill him later. He asks Charlotte if this is true. She says it probably is, but that she will save him.

Chapter 8 – A Talk at Home

Fern tells her mum about conversations the animals have. Her mum starts to worry about her, but her dad puts it down to her lively imagination.

Chapter 9 – Wilbur's Boast

Fern listens to a conversation between Wilbur and Charlotte about spider's legs. Charlotte says she needs them to spin a web, but Wilbur says he bets he could spin one anyway. He has two attempts and gives up. As Wilbur and Charlotte continue to chat, they are interrupted by a lamb that is rude to Wilbur. Charlotte stands up to him and Wilbur checks that she is going to keep her promise about trying to save him. She says she is working on a plan.

Chapter 10 – An Explosion

Charlotte comes up with an idea to play a trick on the Zuckermans. Fern and Avery go to the farm and, when Avery sees Charlotte, he decides to try and get her. Luckily, he falls over the rat's rotten egg, breaks it and causes an awful smell. Everyone talks about how the rat saved Charlotte and Wilbur gives him some of his dinner. Charlotte works on her web.

Chapter 11 – The Miracle

Charlotte spins a web with the words 'some pig' written in the centre of it. Mr Zuckerman sees it and says it's a miracle and that the pig must be special. Word gets around and everyone wants to come and see the pig and the web. Wilbur gets more food.

Chapter 12 – A Meeting

The animals hold a meeting where they are all present except Templeton, the rat. Charlotte explains what has happened but tells them she needs to change the word now. They come up with 'terrific' but Charlotte can't spell it. They then decide to ask Templeton to find a word next time he sees a magazine at the dump. When he appears, Templeton is not keen and says why don't they just let Wilbur die. They remind him of how Wilbur shares his food with him. Templeton finally agrees, but Wilbur starts to worry because he doesn't think he is that terrific.

Chapter 13 – Good Progress
Charlotte works on the web, spinning the word 'terrific' into it. The next day, Mr Zuckerman calls the local paper and Wilbur is given special treats. Templeton keeps looking for words and finally comes back with a soap powder advert with the word 'radiant' on it. Charlotte tells Wilbur stories and Fern listens to them before she goes home.

Chapter 14 – Dr. Dorian
Fern tells her mum about what a good storyteller Charlotte is. Her mother becomes worried about her and so goes to see her doctor. The doctor says that Fern is probably right and that animals do talk to each other. She tells her not to worry.

Chapter 15 – The Crickets
Wilbur turns into a great pig and starts to perform for his visitors but, while he becomes the centre of attention, the fame does not change him. The Zuckermans decide to take him to the fair and Wilbur asks Charlotte to go too. Charlotte says she can't go because she has to lay her eggs and that she won't be able to help Wilbur for much longer as she needs to devote her energy to her eggs.

Chapter 16 – Off to the Fair
Before they head off to the fair, Mrs Zuckerman decides to give Wilbur a buttermilk bath. Charlotte decides to go along and takes Templeton too. Wilbur overhears the adults talking about how he'll make good bacon when they kill him. Wilbur passes out in shock and they pour water over him. They finally set off to the fair.

Chapter 17 – Uncle
They arrive at the fair and Wilbur's crate is placed next to another crate containing a pig called Uncle. Uncle is much bigger than Wilbur, although he, too, is a spring pig. Charlotte is getting tired and Wilbur starts to worry both about her and the fact that the judges will be deciding which pig is best in the show the next day.

Chapter 18 – The Cool of the Evening
Templeton goes exploring and brings back the word 'humble' for Charlotte to spin in her web. She reassures Wilbur that because he is now so famous there is no way they will kill him off. Charlotte spends the rest of the evening doing something for her, but won't tell Wilbur what it is.

1

Chapter 19 – The Egg Sac

When Wilbur wakes up, he sees an egg sac next to Charlotte. She tells him it is full of 514 eggs, but that nothing will happen until next spring. Charlotte tells Wilbur that she is slowing down and is worried that she will not be around next year to see her children. Templeton comes back from his night out and tells them that Uncle has won first prize and that Wilbur will be turned into bacon. Charlotte tells him to ignore him. The next morning, when the family arrives, they see the word 'humble' in the web. Although they are disappointed that Wilbur has not won, they still bathe him in buttermilk. They then hear a message over the loudspeaker system asking Mr Zuckerman to bring Wilbur to the central field for a special prize. Charlotte is content that she has saved Wilbur's life. Meanwhile, Fern's attentions are diverted by a boy called Henry Fussy.

Chapter 20 – The Hour of Triumph

Wilbur faints from excitement when he hears he has won an award for attracting so many visitors to the summer fair. Mr Zuckerman says that he has fainted out of modesty, but he soon wakes up when Templeton bites his tail.

Chapter 21 – Last Day

Wilbur starts to worry about how quiet Charlotte has become. They talk and Charlotte tells him not to worry and that his life is safe. Wilbur gets upset and says he can't understand why he ever thought she was bloodthirsty and asks her why she helped him. Charlotte says it was because she liked him. Wilbur talks excitedly about going home, but Charlotte says she hasn't got enough strength and won't make it. Wilbur says that he won't let her die alone and that he is going to stay with her. Charlotte explains that he can't and so he decides that the least he can do is look after her web sac. He wakes Templeton and makes him help. Templeton rescues the sac and Wilbur puts it in his mouth to keep it safe during the journey home. He says goodbye to Charlotte, who dies alone the next day.

Chapter 22 – A Warm Wind

Back at the barn, Wilbur puts Charlotte's web sac safely in one corner and watches over it as the seasons turn. As spring arrives, Wilbur notices something move and spots a tiny spider creeping from the sac. Once all the spiders emerge, Wilbur watches over them and, as soon as they are old enough, they start to leave. Wilbur gets upset and falls asleep, but wakes to the sound of three spiders saying hello to him. He looks up and sees them where Charlotte's web used to be. They tell Wilbur that they like it in the barn and have decided to stay. Wilbur tells them about their mother and pledges to be friends with them forever. Zuckerman also takes care of Wilbur.

Guided Reading – *Charlotte's Web*

Reading objectives
- To evaluate a book by referring to details and examples in the text.
- To discuss the enduring appeal of established authors and 'classic' texts.
- To distinguish between the author and the narrator, investigating narrative viewpoint and the treatment of different characters, e.g. minor characters, heroes, villains and perspectives on the action from different characters

Session One

Introducing the text
Ask the children to read the blurb on the back of the book. Discuss the following:
- Who and what are the main characters in the story?
- What do you think is the 'dreadful fate' that Charlotte saves Wilbur from?

Point out that the book is one of the most loved children's stories ever and explain to the children that these books are often called classics. Ask the children what this means, ensuring that they gain an understanding that classics have usually been in print for a long time and read by a few generations. To reinforce this, show the children that the book was first published in 1952.

Strategy check
Explain to the children that much of the book is written in dialogue form and that they need to focus on reading with expression in order to develop the identity of the characters.

Independent reading
Ask the children to read to the end of chapter one and to think about how the author uses dialogue to introduce us to the characters.

Return to the text
Discuss the following:
- Why does Fern's father need an axe?
- Why does Fern's father tell her to 'control' herself?
- What argument does Fern use to try to stop him killing the pig?
- Why do you think Mr Arable says he is being foolish for allowing her to keep the pig?
- What does Fern's brother, Avery, call the pig?
- How does Fern feel about having a pig? Use words from the text to support your answer.

Follow-up activity one
Ask the children to read to the end of chapter three and to write the dialogue between Fern and Wilbur, where he tells her what happened when he tried to escape.

Follow-up activity two
Ask the children to read to the end of chapter four and to imagine they are Wilbur. Ask them to write a diary entry for his worst day ever.

Session Two

Response to the text
Discuss the following:

Chapter two
- Describe the relationship between Fern and Wilbur.
- How does Wilbur keep warm at night?
- Why does Mr Arable want to sell Wilbur when he is five weeks old?
- How does Fern respond to this?
- What idea does Fern's mother have?

Chapter three
- Describe Wilbur's new home.
- Does Wilbur like living in the barn? Use words from the text to support your answer.
- How does Wilbur make his escape?
- After his initial excitement, how does Wilbur feel about his escape?
- What do the other animals do while Wilbur is trying to escape?
- How do they manage to catch him?
- How does he feel about being caught? Use words from the text to support your answer.

Chapter four
- What plans did Wilbur have for the day?
- Why does Wilbur start crying?
- Do the animals like Wilbur? How do you know that?
- What makes Wilbur happy later on in the evening?

Strategy check
Ask the children to think about how the author treats the different characters in the book, for example why we feel empathy towards Wilbur and how we respond to the other animals.

Independent reading
Ask the children to read the first five pages of chapter five up to "I think you're beautiful" and to think about how Wilbur must be feeling as he waits for his new friend to appear.

Return to the text

Discuss the following:
- Why is Wilbur cross with Templeton? Do you think he is being fair?
- What do you think Wilbur is thinking about that stops him sleeping?
- How does the sheep respond to Wilbur? Why do you think that is?
- How does the author make us feel about the sheep? Use words from the text to support your answer.
- How does the author make you feel about Wilbur, knowing he is waiting for his friend to appear?
- What are your first impressions of Charlotte? Why?
- What does Wilbur think of Charlotte? Use words from the text to support your answer.

Follow-up activity three

Ask the children to read to the end of chapter five and to write about how they think Charlotte will prove herself to be a loyal friend.

Follow-up activity four

Ask the children to read to the end of the book and to make a mind map of Charlotte.

1 Charlotte's Web (1)

Name .... Date..........

WILBUR'S ESCAPE

Write the dialogue between Fern and Wilbur where he tells her what happened when he tried to escape.

1 Charlotte's Web (2)

Name .... Date...........

WILBUR'S WORST DAY EVER!

Write a diary entry for Wilbur's worst day ever.

Dear Diary,

Year 5 Enjoy Guided Reading © Badger Publishing Ltd.

1 Charlotte's Web (3)

Name .... Date...........

Charlotte – The Loyal Friend

How do you think Charlotte will prove herself to be a loyal friend?

1   Charlotte's Web (4)

Name .... Date..........

All About Charlotte

Make a mind map of Charlotte.

Charlotte

Year 5 Enjoy Guided Reading © Badger Publishing Ltd.

2 Goodnight Mister Tom
by Michelle Magorian

Chapter Synopsis

Chapter 1 – Meeting
Willie Beech is evacuated to Little Weirwold during the war and is taken in by Thomas Oakley, a widower. Very early on, Tom notices bruises on Willie and deduces that he has come from a violent background. Willie continually acts defensively and bears in mind his mother's words, which are that he must be good or people will discover what a wicked boy he is. Willie goes for a walk and meets Mrs Hartridge, one of the local teachers, who seems friendly and kind. He then spots a dog that he thinks is poisonous. He is about to hit it when Tom sees him and tells him not to. Willie responds by thinking he is going to get hit; Tom reassures him he won't. They go inside and prepare Willie's room. The chapter ends with Tom thinking about his wife, who died during childbirth, and his son, who died soon after.

Chapter 2 – Little Weirwold
Tom teaches Willie how to make friends with Sam the dog, but Willie gets confused because he isn't used to people being nice to him. Tom notices even more signs of neglect in the form of welts and goes to ask a neighbour, Mrs Fletcher, to knit a jumper for him, as Willie's clothes are in such bad condition. Tom reads a letter from Willie's mother. She gives Tom permission to hit Willie and encloses a belt for the purpose. Tom reassures Willie he would never use it and gives him a wash and something to eat. He then puts Willie to bed, but notices that he lies under it and not in it. Willie cries because he is so happy.

Chapter 3 – Saturday Morning
Willie wakes up frightened, realising that he has wet the bed, and so hides underneath. In the morning, Mr Tom finds the wet bed and washes the covers. He then tells Willie to write a postcard to his mother, letting her know where he is, and finds that Willie can't read or write and has never painted. He takes Willie to the doctor, who says that he is malnourished and gives him some ointment for the welts.

Chapter 4 – Equipped
Mr Tom takes Willie into town to buy some material for some new clothes. Mr Tom wonders how he managed to get given such a sickly, dependent child. Willie asks if they can go to the artists' shop, but Mr Tom says there isn't time. The truth is that he is reluctant to go there, having not been inside for forty years since his wife, Rachel, died. They join the library and, while Willie is looking at books, Mr Tom decides to go into the artists' shop. Back at home, he puts a rubber sheet on Willie's bed and tells him he's not angry about the bed wetting. At bedtime, he reads to Willie.

2

Chapter 5 - 'Chamberlain Announces'

It is Sunday. Willie wets the bed again and Mr Tom doesn't make a fuss. They go to church and Willie helps to put the hymn books out. They hear on the radio that the country is officially at war and so they go home and build an Anderson Shelter with the help of the Fletcher family. Mr Tom goes out and leaves Willie to fill in the soil, which he does. He also spots a boy that he first saw watching him at the post office.

Chapter 6 – Zach

The boy's name is Zach and he tells Willie that Mr Tom has the reputation of being a bit of a recluse. Zach also says that he liked Willie the first time he saw him and thinks they're alike in that they are both loners. Willie is shocked that someone likes him as his mother says people only like him when he's quiet and invisible. They finish the shelter together. Meanwhile, much to the surprise of the other villagers, Mr Tom goes to the village meeting and offers to be a special constable. He goes home and meets Zach, who is staying at the doctor's house. He gives Willie a bath, something he's never had before, and reads him a story.

Chapter 7 – An Encounter over Blackberries

For the first time ever, Willie experiences excitement, but this scares him as his mother says it's a sin. Zach calls for Willie as does George, whose mum says she is making a picnic so George and his twin sisters can go blackberrying. They all go and, although it is a bit strained to start with, particularly when they ask Willie what he likes doing and Willie can't think of anything until he suddenly remembers drawing, the day is a success. When Willie gets home, he sees that Mr Tom has made the shelter homely and they go inside to make jam together. Willie goes to bed happy that he has survived a day with four other people his own age.

Chapter 8 – School

It is Willie's first day at school and he gets upset because he can't read, means he isn't put in the same class as the twins and Zach. When he tells Mr Tom what's happened, Mr Tom promises to help him learn and they agree to practise every morning before school. They start by practising his name, which he does well, and Mr Tom is impressed by Willie's ability to draw. George, the twins and later Zach, go to Willie's house and say that, although they are upset he is not in their class, they still want to be his friend. They all arrange to go to the woods on Saturday.

2

Chapter 9 – Birthday Boy

It is Willie's birthday and Mr Tom is surprised by Willie's reaction to his 'Happy Birthday' greeting and the fact that he doesn't ask if the post has come. They practise writing and then Willie goes for his morning run with Sam. The postman arrives and Mr Tom is surprised that there is no post from London. He then lays out a birthday breakfast for Willie, where there are presents from Mr Tom and people from the village. When Willie comes home, he can't quite believe it and opens his presents. He gets clothes from Mr Tom, a book from the librarian and an art set from Mr Tom, who realised that going to the art shop wasn't as painful as he imagined it would be. After school, Willie goes to thank his neighbours and Mr Tom tells him to go to the church to do some sketching. Zach comes in amazed at his artwork and takes him home, where a surprise birthday tea awaits him with more friends and presents. At bedtime, Willie is sick due to the excitement of it all.

Chapter 10 – The Case

The war is beginning to have an effect on the village. Zach gets a case from home and in it finds his tap shoes, clothes and a letter from his parents. Willie's friendships grow stronger but the group of friends start to worry that there isn't anywhere they can go to play. Willie, worriedly, suggests Mr Tom's, but needs to go home and check whether Mr Tom minds. Once at home, Willie practises his reading and writing and Emilia Thorne, the librarian, helps too. Mr Tom notices Willie is quiet and asks him what's troubling him. Willie asks if his friends can come and play in his room and Mr Tom says yes. Willie agrees to clear up any mess that is made and they decide not to tell anyone about the bed wetting.

Chapter 11 – Friday

Mr Tom talks to Mrs Fletcher about how Willie has been with him for almost two months and how he saw him laugh for the first time. He concludes that Willie is better off there than with his mother. Mrs Fletcher thinks about the positive effect Willie has had on Mr Tom. Willie's reading is progressing well and his teacher has told him he can move on to joined up handwriting. George, Zach and the twins come round and talk about ideas they have had for writing their own Gazette newspaper and other plans for Christmas plays and concerts. Willie finds himself volunteering for things. The friends have a good time and Mr Tom brings up drinks and snacks for them. Zach tells Willie he is lucky to be with Mr Tom and Willie says he knows. When the friends leave, Willie goes to see Mr Tom. Most of his scars have healed and he goes to bed. When he wakes up his sheets are dry.

2

Chapter 12 – The Show Must Go On

The war continues, but most of the evacuees go home. Willie's reading is now up to standard and the gazette is completed – mainly by Willie and Carrie. Willie helps out as a prompt at the Christmas play rehearsals but, because two of the evacuees are missing, he ends up having to stand in for one of them. He does very well and, while everyone is congratulating him, Emilia Thorne finds out that the two children have gone home. Again Willie has to step in, this time as Scrooge. When he gets home, he finds Mr Tom agitated. The teacher who was going to play the organ for the Christmas carol concert has been called up and Mr Tom has been asked to step in and play. He tells Willie he hasn't played since his wife died. He also tells Willie he had a son called William.

Chapter 13 – Carol Singing

The choir has a carol practice and everyone compliments Mr Tom on his excellent playing and thanks him for a good rehearsal. Once everyone has left, Mr Tom plays Willie a tune his wife loved and Willie is moved to tears. Mr Tom says he enjoyed playing.

Chapter 14 – New Beginnings

Everything is going well for Willie and his friends, apart from Lucy, who is upset that Willie has been moved up into Mrs Hartridge's class. Carrie decides she wants to try for a scholarship to the grammar school and asks Mrs Hartridge to talk to her parents because she will be the first girl to do it. After school, Willie and his friends attend a meeting about the next production, which is to be Toad of Toad Hall. When Willie gets home, Mr Tom tells him he has received a letter from his mother and that she wants him to go home because she isn't well.

Chapter 15 – Home

After a sad farewell at the train station between Willie and Mr Tom, Willie departs for London. His mother meets him at the station but she doesn't recognise him. Willie then tries to help his mother but she hits him, but then decides to be nice to him before he has to accept his new responsibilities. She becomes unnerved when he smiles and realises it will take her a day or so to make him obedient again. When Willie tells her he has brought some presents from the people in the village, she accuses him of lying and says that they're probably glad he's gone. Willie tells her they liked him, but starts to feel as if he is two people and knows that his mother won't like the new William. She tells him they have to creep home so no one notices them. Inside the house, he sees a baby in a box on a chair. Her mouth is taped up, which, his mother says, is so that she isn't heard by anyone. Willie unpacks his new clothes and gives his mother a drawing he made of the church. She says that he has stolen everything, hits him and locks him under the stairs. When he wakes up, he is covered with bruises and smells. She has taken his boots and sewn his vest into his underpants.

2

Chapter 16 – The Search

Mr Tom misses Willie and, after three weeks and no letters from him, becomes very anxious about him. One night, he has a nightmare that he was locked in a tiny space and could hear Willie calling for help. There is other bad news in the village in the form of a telegram for Mrs Hartridge and, when Mr Tom hears of it, he goes to get Mrs Fletcher, whose son also died in the war. Mr Tom decides to get a train to London to check on Willie and Sam follows him. Once in London, he travels to Deptford and, when the siren goes off, heads for the shelter. He talks to a warden and tells him he's looking for Willie, but the warden says he hasn't seen Willie since last September.

They talk to a neighbour, who tells Mr Tom that Willie's mother has gone to the coast and that Willie was sent back because of his bad behaviour. They go to the house and Sam smells something. The police break down the door and there is a bad stench as if someone has died.

Chapter 17 – Rescue

They find Willie tied up and covered in bruises, sores and excrement. He is holding the baby in his arms and won't let go of her. Mr Tom has to wait outside and, when they allow him in, they tell him that Willie is settled and that he has seen a psychologist who has recommended he go to a children's home. Mr Tom is allowed to see Willie for a few minutes and then a psychologist, who tells Mr Tom that, because he is not a relative, he has no say in the matter. Mr Tom talks to Rachel, who says she would kidnap him, and Mr Tom decides to do so. He takes him that night, wraps him up and gets a train to a village near to Little Weirwold. He then walks and hitches the rest of the way. Back at home, he takes Willie to see the doctor, who says that the authorities will eventually trace Willie. He examines Willie and says the scars will heal but inside he has emotional problems. Zach is pleased to see Mr Tom and Willie and says he will do all he can to help.

Chapter 18 – 'Recovery'

Willie continually has nightmares and Mr Tom tells him to scream all he needs to. He is in a feverish state and Mr Tom is frightened to leave him. One morning, he wakes up better and Zach visits. He tells Willie that Mrs Hartridge has had a baby. Willie realises that a man is needed for a baby and that his mother has been lying to him. He talks to Mr Tom about this and Mr Tom says that his mother is sick. Willie says he doesn't want to go back and that he missed Mr Tom. He tells him he loves him and Mr Tom tells Willie he loves him too. Willie starts to get better and goes to visit Mrs Hartridge. He watches her feed the baby and realises it wasn't his fault his baby sister died.

Chapter 19 – The Sea, the Sea, the Sea!

Mr Tom takes Will, as he now wants to be known, and Zach to the seaside. They have a great time and Will learns to swim. Towards the end of the holiday, Zach worries when he hears that London has been blitzed, but finds out his parents are safe. They go home to the news that Carrie has passed her scholarship exam to grammar school.

Chapter 20 – Spooky Cott

Zach, Will, George and the twins go to Spooky Cott. They get scared because they hear sounds and, apart from Will and Zach, the other three run away. A man appears and it turns out that he is from a local convalescent home. He tells them his name is Geoffrey and he is an amputee as a result of a bomb blast in London. Zach makes Will show him a drawing and the man, an artist, tells Will he has a real gift. They tell him that they go to the local school, but that there are not enough teachers, and he says he will try to teach there. When Will gets home, he finds Mr Tom in the sitting room with four other people. Mr Tom tells him that his mother has committed suicide and that the people want to put him in a children's home. Will says if they do that he will run away and that he wants to stay with Tom. The adults talk and finally agree that Mr Tom can adopt him.

Chapter 21 – Back to School

It is the first day of school. Carrie goes to the grammar school and, when the others get to class, they see that Geoffrey is one of their teachers. Zach is called out of class and told that his father has been injured in a blast. He insists on going to London to see him and, while he is away, Will celebrates his tenth birthday. He receives a book written by Zach. In it Zach has written an inscription saying he will write the next part on his return. Reports come in that the bombing on London gets worse and they then receive word that Zach has been killed.

Chapter 22 – Grieving

Will finds it hard to accept that Zach is dead and cannot deal with it. One day, he goes to see Geoffrey for an art lesson. Geoffrey gives Will a picture of his best friend, who has also died, and asks him to draw him. Will starts to think about Zach and goes off on his own. When he arrives home late, he apologises to Mr Tom, calling him Dad. Will takes Zach's bike and learns to ride it, and then goes to see Mrs Hartridge, who had just heard that her husband has been traced and is a prisoner of war. Will takes part in the play and is a great success.

Guided Reading – *Goodnight Mister Tom*

Reading objectives
- To investigate how characters are presented, referring to the text: through dialogue, action and description; how the reader responds to them (as victims, heroes); through examining their relationships with other characters.
- To evaluate a book by referring to details and examples in the text.
- To distinguish between the author and the narrator, investigating narrative viewpoint and the treatment of different characters.

Session One

Introducing the text
Ask the children to read the blurb and consider what the word 'evacuated' means. Ask them if they know of anyone, perhaps grandparents, who were evacuated in the Second World War. Through reading the blurb, ask them to think about the state Willie was in when he was evacuated and how he has flourished in his new surroundings. Draw out the conclusion that many children didn't want to be evacuated because it meant leaving their family behind whereas, for Willie, we can deduce that it was a positive experience.

Strategy check
While reading the book, ask the children to focus on how the author portrays the character of Willie and how we respond to him.

Independent reading
Ask the children to read chapter one and to think about what it tells us about Willie's upbringing in London.

Return to the text
Discuss the following:
- Describe Mr Tom.
- What first impression did you make of Mr Tom from his encounter with the Billeting Officer? Use evidence from the text to support your answer.
- How does Willie feel when he enters the house?
- How would you describe Willie's background? Use words from the text to help you.
- How would Willie describe himself? Who has made him feel like that?
- How is Mrs Hartridge different from Willie's teacher in London?
- Why does Willie go to hit the dog?
- Why does Willie start to feel sick?
- Does Mr Tom agree with beating children? How do you know?
- What do we learn about Mr Tom by the end of the chapter? Does your impression of him change?

Follow-up activity one
Ask the children to read to the end of chapter three and to write a character profile on Willie.

Follow-up activity two
Explain to the children you want them to read to the end of chapter eight and to make notes on how life changes for both Mr Tom and Willie.

Session Two

Response to the text
Discuss the following:
Chapter two
- How does Willie respond to Mr Tom being so nice? Why do you think that is?
- Why does Mr Tom ask Mrs Fletcher about her knitting?
- What does the letter from Willie's mum say? How does Mr Tom respond to it? Use words from the text to help you answer.
- Why do you think Willie gets under the bed?
- Why does Willie cry when he is in bed?

Chapter three
- How does Mr Tom respond when Willie wets the bed?
- Why do you think Willie wets the bed?
- What do we learn about Willie in this chapter?
- What is the doctor's diagnosis of Willie?

Chapter four
- Do you think Mr Tom is beginning to enjoy having Willie stay with him? Why do you think that? Use words from the text to help you with your answer.
- How do you think Willie feels when Mr Tom buys him lots of clothes?
- Why is Mr Tom so reluctant to go to the artists' shop?
- What is it about Mr Tom that surprises Miss Thorne when he goes into the library?
- What does it say about Willie that he asks Mr Tom to help him learn to read?

Chapter five
- What is an Anderson Shelter and why do they need one?
- Why does Mr Tom say Willie has got a temperature?
- Who does Willie meet at the end of the chapter?

2

Chapter six
- How does Zach describe Mr Tom?
- Why is Willie so surprised that someone likes him?
- Why is everyone surprised when Mr Tom turns up at the meeting?
- Why does Willie have such a strange reaction to the bath tub?

Chapter seven
- What emotion does Willie feel for the first time?
- Why is Willie upset when Sam beats him in a race?
- Why does Willie respond strangely when Mr Tom tells him to go and play?
- Why is Willie so relieved when the day is over?

Chapter eight
- Why is Willie put into a different class than his friends? How does this make him feel?
- How does Mr Tom help Willie?
- Why is Mr Tom so impressed?
- Who do you think told Willie he would go to hell if he copied things?
- How do Willie's friends cheer him up?

Strategy check

Again ask the children to think about how the author has portrayed both Mr Tom and Willie. Ask them to consider whether her treatment of them has altered as the book progresses, for example, do we still see Willie as so much of a victim?

Independent reading

Ask the children to read chapter nine, Birthday Boy, and to consider the way Willie reacts to having a birthday.

Return to the text

Discuss the following:
- Is Mr Tom surprised that there is no post from London? Why do you think that?
- How does Willie respond to his birthday? Why does this surprise Mr Tom so much?
- What words does the author use to convey Willie's response to his presents?
- Why does the occasion remind Mr Tom of Rachel? What does this tell us about the way he is changing?
- How do we know Willie's drawing is of an excellent standard? Use words from the text to support your answer.
- Why do you think Willie gets sick after his birthday tea?

Follow-up activity three
Explain to the children that you want them to read to the end of chapter fourteen and to write the next part of the story about when Willie and his mum meet. Ask them to consider how Willie must be feeling, whether she really is ill and whether she will be proud of Willie when she sees him.

Follow-up activity four
Ask the children to read to the end of the book and to choose an important event or incident that takes place in the book. Ask them to think about why it is so important to the plot and how it affects either Mr Tom or Willie or both.

2 Goodnight Mister Tom (1)

Name .... Date...........

WILLIE BEECH

Write a character profile on Willie.

Year 5 Enjoy Guided Reading © Badger Publishing Ltd.

2 Goodnight Mister Tom (2)

Name .... Date ....

MR TOM AND WILLIE

Make notes on how life changes for both Mr Tom and Willie.

Mr Tom

Willie

2 Goodnight Mister Tom (3)

Name .... Date...........

MEETING MUM

Write the next part of the story about when Willie and his mum meet. Think about how Willie must be feeling, whether she really is ill and whether she will be proud of Willie when she sees him.

2 Goodnight Mister Tom (4)

Name .... Date............

An Important Event

Choose an important event or incident that takes place in the book. Think about why it is so important to the plot and how it affects either Mr Tom or Willie or both.

My event is

Why is it important to the plot?

How does it affect Mr Tom or Willie or both or them?

Year 5 Enjoy Guided Reading © Badger Publishing Ltd.

3 The Illustrated Mum *by Jacqueline Wilson*

Chapter Synopsis

Chapter 1 – Cross

Dolphin and Star live with their mum, Marigold, who suffers from bouts of depression. It is her birthday and they make her cards and give her presents and Marigold, who is already covered in tattoos, decides that she wants another one – although she has promised the girls she won't have any more. Marigold is quite tearful and spends much of her life dreaming of Micky, Star's dad, hoping he will return. As Star develops into a teenager, she is finding her relationship with Marigold increasingly difficult and wishes she was more like a normal mother. Marigold decides to go out and celebrate her birthday, promising she'll be back by 10.30. When the girls go to bed at midnight, Marigold hasn't yet returned.

Chapter 2 – Marigold

The girls wake up early and Dol decides to see if Marigold is home. She is frightened when she realises she is not there and climbs into bed with Star until it's time to get ready for school. On the way to school, Star, who is increasingly becoming the adult of the family, tells Dol not to say anything about Marigold because they don't want the social workers involved. Dol has a bad day at school; she's bullied and no one wants to play with her. At the end of the school day, she walks to Star's high school and waits for her sister there. They walk home together, worried that something has happened to Marigold.

Chapter 3 – Dolphin

Marigold is back and, by way of apology, is baking biscuits and cakes for the girls. Star is angry with her but Dol is just relieved to see her. When Star storms off to do her homework, Dol asks her where she's been. Marigold tells her she went to a party. Star goes out to McDonald's and, when Dol asks if she can go too, she says that little sisters aren't allowed to hang around. Dol stays in with Marigold and eats cakes while her mother drinks vodka, but tells her not to mention it to Star. Marigold asks her who her friends are at school and Dol says she hasn't got any but would like to be friends with Tasha. When Star comes home, the girls go to bed and talk about how Marigold is getting "manic" again. The next day, Marigold turns up at Dol's school and invites Tasha home for tea. Both Tasha and her mum are horrified by the suggestion and rush away.

Chapter 4 – Daisy Chain

Marigold suggests going to meet Star after school, but Dol dissuades her as she knows Star would be horrified. She then offers to buy Dol some new clothes and flashes a new credit card at her. This worries Dol too and she suggests that they just go for a walk and a picnic. They play make-believe games and Marigold tells Dol how she was brought up in a home and longed for a sister.

Dol starts to worry about Star and tells Marigold that they'll have to get a bus home. At the bus stop, Marigold sees a poster advertising an Emerald City reunion concert. Marigold gets excited as they were her and Micky's favourite band.

Chapter 5 – Heart

When they get home, Star is angry. Dol has a nightmare and, when Star won't let her get in bed with her, she goes to see Marigold, who is slumped over the kitchen table, drunk. The next day, Dol has to wash at school because Marigold is in the bathroom, being sick. The girls in her class taunt her that she lives in a squat which, although she has done in the past, she isn't now. She hits one of the girls, gets told off and spends lunchtime hiding in the library. Mr Hargreaves, the teacher in the library, is friendly to her and Owly, one of the boys from her class, comes in and they make friends. His real name is Oliver, he thinks Marigold is great and tells Dol that his mum has suffered from moods since his dad left. He asks if he can go to Dol's house for tea. When Dol and Star get home, they find Marigold dressed up. She tells them she's going to the Emerald City concert, hoping to meet Micky.

Chapter 6 – Star

Star is sceptical about Micky and angry with Marigold. Dol asks her why she's so angry, because she is Marigold's favourite. She then tells Dol that she has got a boyfriend and wanted to go and meet him. Dol tells her to go and she does, but she comes back feeling guilty about leaving Dol on her own. Dol goes with her and tells her she doesn't like how Star is with Mark. Marigold comes in late and wakes the girls up to introduce them to Micky.

Chapter 7 – Sorceress

Star is shocked to meet Micky, who didn't know he had a daughter. They stare at each other and Dol feels left out of the family unit. He notices that Marigold is drunk and buys them all a pizza. After they have eaten, he asks Star if he can see her again and Marigold is shocked that he is leaving, having convinced herself that their relationship would start up again. Star asks him to stay and he does. The next day, he takes them all out for breakfast and then buys them all presents. He is very proud of Star, takes his new role seriously and acts concerned at the way Marigold is behaving.

Chapter 8 – Eye

Micky keeps in contact and sends all three of them presents, including a mobile phone. One day, he sends two children's tickets to Brighton for Star and Dol. Marigold insists on going, but Star says she can't and that Micky has a girlfriend. Dol decides to stay with Marigold and Star leaves. Star rings her from the station and asks her if she's changed her mind, but she hasn't.

3

Finally Marigold decides they should go to Brighton to search for Micky, but they have no luck. Dol gets tired and wants to go home, but Marigold gets cross with her and hits her. Dol assumes the adult role and persuades Marigold to go home. Back at home, Star rings and tells Dol that Micky is worried about her and that she shouldn't have to look after Marigold.

Chapter 9 – Serpent

Micky drives Star home but he doesn't come in. Marigold is nice to Star about her weekend with Micky, but Star is convinced she has an ulterior motive. In bed, Star and Dol talk about the weekend and Star tells her that she is thinking of going to live with Micky and that they want her to go too. Dol worries about Marigold, but Star says she needs professional help. Marigold seems happier during the week and Oliver comes to tea. On Friday, Marigold asks Star if she is going to Brighton; she says she is and Marigold says that she and Dol might go too. Star says she can't and she starts drinking again. In bed, Star tries to persuade Dol to go with her, but when Dol sees that she has packed two bags, she realises she isn't coming back. Dol won't leave Marigold and, when she wakes up at six o'clock the following morning, Star has gone.

Chapter 10 – Bats

Marigold thinks that Star will be back on Sunday and so decides to take Dol on a spending spree, buying new clothes for all of them and paint for Star and Dol's bedroom. On Sunday, when Star calls to say she isn't coming back, Marigold starts drinking and Dol has to get herself ready for school the next day. Star calls and, in an attempt to get her to come home, Dol lies and tells her that Marigold tried to hit her, smashed the phone and is now in a coma. Marigold snatches the phone from her and tells her she's lying. Dol gets up in the night and finds Marigold in the bathroom, painting herself white.

Chapter 11 – Frog

When Dol tries to get the paint off and can't, she realises that she will have to call an ambulance. The ambulance comes and takes Marigold to hospital and Dol lies, saying that her dad is on his way home to look after her. She goes to school, tells Oliver what has happened and asks if she can stay with him for a couple of nights until Marigold is out of hospital. His mother says no and Oliver says they should try to trace her dad. All Dol knows about him is that his name was Micky and he was a lifeguard. Oliver traces a Micky, now known as Michael, and asks him if he knows a Marigold, which he does.

Chapter 12 – Scream

Dol is nervous about speaking to her dad and makes Oliver hang up. He finally persuades Dol to go and meet him, so they bunk the afternoon off school and go and see him. When they get there, he thinks Oliver is his son and then tells them he is married with two daughters.

He tells Dol he will take care of her, but he will need to talk to his wife first. He explains that he lived with Marigold and Star for eleven months and then Marigold ran away. He searched for her, but never found her. He drives Oliver home and takes Dol to see Marigold. Marigold won't talk to her and Dol leaves, upset.

Chapter 13 – Diamonds

Although Michael says he will take care of Dol, he calls social services because he decides that it would be better to do things through the proper channels. Dol is taken to a foster home, where she meets her foster mother, Aunty Jane. Aunty Jane is very welcoming and kind and doesn't get cross when Dol wets the bed. When Dol says she doesn't want to go to school the next day, Aunty Jane makes her go and takes her there. The teachers are nice to her and Dol rushes out at the end of school to visit Marigold. Aunty Jane is waiting for her and says that Michael will take her to the hospital later. Michael tells her that his family want to meet her and invites her over on Sunday. When she tells him she's dyslexic, he promises to help her learn to read and also to swim. He also says that he has spoken to his doctor, who has explained all about manic depression. Back at Aunty Jane's, Dol gets a surprise when Star turns up to stay too.

Chapter 14 – The Full Picture

Star and Dol have a big row, which ends in Star saying she was really worried about her and so made Micky bring her up to London. She says that Micky hasn't abandoned her but, because the social services are involved, Star has been put in a foster home too. They go to see Marigold and the nurse tells them that, as long as she takes her tablets, she will soon be home with her girls. Marigold tells the girls that she has been attending therapy sessions and realises that she has been treating the two of them in the same way as her mother treated her. Dol realises how much Marigold loves them both and knows that they will be alright in the end.

Guided Reading – *The Illustrated Mum*

Reading objectives

- To investigate how characters are presented, referring to the text: through dialogue, action and description; how the reader responds to them (as victims, heroes); through examining their relationships with other characters.
- To develop an active attitude towards reading: seeking answers, anticipating events, empathising with characters and imagining events that are described.
- To identify the point of view from which the story is told and how this affects the reader's response.

3

Session One

Introducing the text
Talk to the children about Jacqueline Wilson as an author. Ask the children if they have read any of her other work and, if so, what sort of issues she raises. Explain to them that this book is about two girls and their mother, who sometimes suffers from an illness called depression. Ask the children if they know what depression is and, as they read the book, to consider the effect it has on the two girls and their mother.

Strategy check
Ask the children to read the first two paragraphs of the book and, in conjunction with the blurb on the back, to identify the point of view from which the story is written. Ask them to bear this in mind when they are reading the book and to consider whether this affects their response to the book in any way.

Independent reading
Ask the children to continue to read the first chapter up to "...You promised." (page 12) Explain to them that you want them to think about what life is like for Star and Dol.

Return to the text
Discuss the following:
- What do you think Dol means when she says that Marigold is starting going 'weird' again?
- Why do you think Marigold started crying on her birthday?
- How do you think Dol feels when Marigold says she should have drawn "mumsie" things?
- Does Dol have many friends at school? How do you know?
- What do we learn about Marigold's background?
- How does Marigold feel about herself as a mother?
- How does Dol respond to Marigold's depression? Use examples from the text to support your answer.
- Who is Micky? Do you think he will come back? Why do you think that?
- How does Star respond to Marigold wanting another tattoo?

Follow-up activity one
Ask the children to read to the end of the second chapter on Marigold and to then write a diary entry for Dol's day. Remind the children to think about how Dol is treated by the others in her class and how worried she is about Marigold.

Follow-up activity two
Explain to the children that you want them to read to the end of chapter six – Star and to make notes on the girls' lives.

3

Session Two

Response to the text

Discuss the following:

Chapter two
- How do the girls feel when they realise that Marigold hasn't come home?
- Who takes on the role of adult? Do you think this is fair?
- Do you think Marigold was right to stay out all night?
- Have you ever been left on your own? How would or did you feel?
- Why does Star tell Dol not to mention the fact that Marigold didn't come home?
- Do you think the way Miss Hill treats Dol is fair? How do you think she should treat her?

Chapter three
- Describe the ways in which the two girls respond to finding Marigold at home?
- Why do you think Star is so cross?
- Why do you think Marigold wants to bake biscuits and cakes for the girls?
- Do you think Marigold can help behaving in that way?
- How does Dol feel when Marigold collects her from school and tries to invite Tasha for tea?
- Why do you think Marigold did it?

Chapter four
- Why is Dol worried about Marigold having a credit card?
- Why do you think Marigold and Dol enjoy playing pretend games?
- Who should be worried about Star and why?
- Why does Marigold get excited at the bus stop?
- Why does Dol get worried at the bus stop?

Chapter five
- Who comforts Dol when she has a nightmare?
- Why does Dol have to wash at school?
- Do you think Dol was right to punch Kayleigh? Why do you think that?
- Why does Dol go to the library?
- Why do you think Owly Morris and Dol strike up a friendship?
- Why is Marigold so keen to go to the Emerald City concert?

3

Chapter six
- Do you think Star is right to be unsure about Marigold meeting up with Micky?
- Why does Star come back?
- Why is Dol worried about Star?
- Who does Marigold come home with?

Strategy check
Encourage the children to think about who are the victims and the heroes in the story. Ask them to decide whether Marigold is a hero or a victim and what affect having the story told from Dol's perspective has on it.

Independent reading
Ask the children to read the first six pages of chapter 7 – Sorceress up to '"Please stay," she whispered.' Ask the children to note down words from the text that are used to show the reaction that Star and Micky have towards each other.

Return to the text
Discuss the following:
- Describe Micky.
- What words does the author use to describe the reaction Star and Micky have towards one another?
- How does Dol feel? Use words from the text to support your answer.
- What do you think Marigold hopes will happen now she has met Micky again?
- How does Micky feel about finding out that he is a father?
- How do you think Micky feels about the amount Marigold is drinking? How do you know that?

Follow-up activity three
Explain to the children that you want them to read to the end of chapter nine – Serpent and to write the next part of the story about what Marigold will do when she finds out that Star isn't coming back.

Follow-up activity four
Ask the children to read to the end of the book and, as they do so, to make notes on how life improves for Star and Dol.

35

3   The Illustrated Mum (1)

Name .... Date...........

My Day by Dol

Write a diary entry for Dol's day. Remember to think about how Dol is treated by the others in her class and how worried she is about Marigold.

Dear Diary,

Year 5 Enjoy Guided Reading © Badger Publishing Ltd.

3. The Illustrated Mum (2)

Name .... Date............

Our Lives

Read to the end of chapter six – Star and make notes on Dol's and Star's lives.

//
3 The Illustrated Mum (3)

Name .... Date............

What Will Marigold Do Next?

Write the next part of the story about what you think Marigold will do when she finds out that Star isn't coming back.

3 The Illustrated Mum (4)

Name .... Date...........

How Life Changes

Read to the end of the book and make notes on how life improves for Star and Dol.

4 Seasons of Splendour *by Madhur Jaffrey*

Story Synopsis

Savitri and Satyavan

Savitri is a princess and, when she comes of age, her parents tell her she must marry. They let her choose a suitor, but the man she falls in love with, Satyavan, is poor and lives in the forest with his blind parents. When Satyavan tells his parents he loves her, but that he has nothing to offer her, they tell him that they had a kingdom once but that it was stolen from them by the king's brother. Satyavan then agrees to the wedding. On their wedding day, a sage tells the princess that Satyavan will die soon but that, if she eats fruits and leaves, he will survive a year. Savitri does this and, on the day he is destined to die, she insists on going to the forest with him. He complains of a headache, so they sit under the banyan tree and he dies. Savitri prays to the banyan tree to save her husband and waits for Yamraj, the King of the Underworld, to claim his soul. She follows him and he gives her a wish, as long as it is not to save Satyavan's soul, so she asks for her in-laws to have their sight returned. She continues to follow him and this time she asks for them to have their kingdom back. This too is granted, but she continues to follow Yamraj. This time her wish is to be the mother of many sons. Yamraj grants this wish too, but cannot understand it when she still follows him. She tells him that he has granted this wish, but that it is a false wish because her husband has died. He finally gives her back her husband and she returns to the banyan tree, where he wakes up. She gives thanks to the banyan tree.

Shravan Kumar and his Wife

Shravan is a good man but his wife can be bad. She treats his parents badly and doesn't like living with them. She cooks two meals, a tasty one for her and Shravan and a sour dish for her in-laws. Her in-laws finally complain to Shravan and he tells her to cook the same meals, which she does for a while. She then orders a cooking pot with two stomachs and cooks different meals again. Again Shravan finds out and takes his parents on a pilgrimage, but won't allow her to accompany them. He carries them in a basket but, when he stops for water, he gets wounded by an arrow charged by King Dashrat. He tells the king to look after his parents, but they are so upset that they demand a funeral pyre is built for them. His parents die and word is sent to Shravan's wife, who rushes to his side. When she finds her husband, she realises that, if the arrow doesn't kill him, the heat will. She begs for shade from the banyan tree, which takes pity on her, saying that she was a bad daughter-in-law but a good wife. Shravan is cured and she is never cruel again.

4

The Birth of Krishna, the Blue God

Wicked King Kans rules over Mathura after putting his father in prison. He has a sister called Devaki who, when she is old enough, he matches with a man called Vasudev. On the day of the wedding, a wise man tells Kans that he should not let the couple leave or he will, one day, die at the hands of their son. He imprisons them and, when they have a daughter, he goes into their cell and drops the baby. As the baby dies, he sees lightning and hears a voice saying that he has done an evil thing, but that she was not the one who will kill him and her brother is yet to be born. The same incident is repeated six times until, one day, Devaki gives birth to a son, Krishna. When he is born, a voice tells Vasudev to take the baby and exchange it with his sister's daughter. The prison cell opens up and Vasudev does as he has been told. Kans hears another daughter has been born and kills the baby, but this time the voice tells him that a son has been born and is safe. Kans vows he will get the son and orders that all boys under twelve months in his kingdom are killed. What he does not realise is that Krishna is safe within another kingdom.

Krishna and the Demon Nurse

Kans is told where Krishna is and that the family is looking for a nurse, so he asks Pootana, the evil demon, to transform herself into a pretty girl, get the job and find a way to kill Krishna. She does this and, one day when Krishna's foster mother is ill, she offers to breast-feed the baby. She puts poison on her nipples, hoping to kill him, but Krishna sucks the life out of her and kills her.

The Serpent King

Kaliya, the serpent king with five heads and of great strength, has been causing widespread destruction to the extent that the cowherds tell Krishna that he has to be stopped. Krishna takes his friends to the water's edge where Kaliya lives. The two fight and Krishna crushes Kaliya to death.

How Krishna Killed the Wicked King Kans

Kans thinks that all his enemies have been destroyed and calls for a week of celebrations. He thinks that Krishna has been killed, but is told otherwise. Kans decides to kill Krishna and does this by issuing a challenge to all wrestlers to fight the court wrestlers. Krishna and his foster brother, Balram, accept the challenge. Once in the ring, Kans lets loose a wild elephant but Krishna manages to sit on its back and kill it. The wrestlers are then sent in and Krishna and Balram kill them. Krishna jumps on the throne, pulls Kans off and tells him he will die. He then frees his grandfather and parents from jail.

Doda and Dodi

Doda and Dodi are brother and sister but, where he is rich, she is poor. On the anniversary of their father's death, Doda decides to go to the holy city, but tells his wife to care for Dodi and her family. His wife sends a strange invitation to Dodi to attend a memorial for her father, but this makes her unsure as to whether her family are really welcome. They go and Dodi helps prepare the food but, once the priests are fed, she and her family are not offered food. Her children are hungry and, in the middle of the night, Dodi wakes up and goes to the kitchen, where she is tempted to steal some bread, but at the last minute changes her mind. They go home and sleep. Dodi dreams of rice pudding and wakes up to the smell of it in her house. She feels her father is watching over her, gets up and finds food and jewels. Meanwhile, in the holy city, Doda goes to offer water to the priests and finds that blood pours out instead. He realises that his sister has been maltreated by his wife and goes home.

Now rich, Dodi invites her sister in-law for dinner. Her sister in-law takes a pot that she fills with dung and, when Dodi asks her what is in the pot, she lies and says yoghurt. Dodi pours it out and finds it is yoghurt, another sign that her father wouldn't want shame brought on the family. When Doda arrives home, he asks his wife if she maltreated Dodi and she says she went there for dinner and then, before taking to her bed and pretending to be ill, she asks Doda to take one cooking pot to her mother and one to Dodi. Doda, realising what his wife is like, swaps the pots and Dodi receives sweets while his mother-in-law receives a pot with scorpions in. Doda's wife seems to be getting worse but, one day, a neighbour asks him to watch his wife from their house. He watches her get up and behave normally. When he gets home, she tells him a doctor came that day and told her of a cure. She says that Dodi and her family must shave their heads and blacken their faces and walk past her house. He says he will organise it but gets his wife's mother and family to do it instead. She is finally humiliated to see her family walk by in this fashion and vows never to be so wicked again.

How Ram Defeated the Demon King Ravan

1. King Dashrat's Special Heir

King Dashrat has three wives but no heir and so he decides to offer up prayers to the gods. The gods decide to grant his wish because the demon king, Ravan, had once requested that no god in heaven or creature in the underworld would kill him and, for some reason, the gods had agreed and now Ravan was out of control. They grant the king four heirs. Ram, his first heir, grows and meets Sita, who he marries.

4

2. Ram is Banished

King Dashrat decides it is time for him to abdicate in favour of his first born and favourite, Ram. However, another of his wives, Kaikeyi, wants her son, Bharat, to be king and so reminds Dashrat of the time she saved his life and he granted her two wishes in return. She tells him she wishes for her son to be made king and for Ram to be banished for fourteen years. The king has to agree and Ram is banished. Sita goes with him, as does another of Ram's brothers, Laxshman, but Bharat is angry with his mother for what she has done and pleads with Ram to stay. The king dies and Ram honours his father's promise.

3. The Kidnapping of Sita

The demon Ravan's sister falls in love with Ram and, when the feeling is not reciprocated, she goes to Ravan for help. He decides to kidnap Sita by tempting her with a golden deer. She sees the deer and Ram goes to catch it for her, but realises it is a trap. The demon lets out a cry and Sita is convinced Ram is injured, so sends Laxshman to help him. While they are away, Sita is kidnapped.

4. The Search for Sita

Sita is taken in a chariot and she drops jewels in the hope that they will help Ram find her. Ram, in despair, asks the monkeys to help him. Hanuman goes in search of Sita and Ram gives him a ring to show Sita so that she realises the monkey is there to help her. He finally finds Sita in Lanka.

5. The Siege of Lanka

Hanuman finds Sita imprisoned in Ravan's home. He shows her Ram's ring and she sends a pearl back. Ram goes to Lanka to find Sita, he kills Ravan and rescues her. The fourteen years of exile are over and he returns home to be crowned king.

The Moon and the Heavenly Nectar

In the beginning of time, the oceans were filled with milk and jewels continually popped out of them. They also contained the heavenly Nectar of Immortality and poison and, when the poison was released by Shiva, the water turned into salt water. Everybody wanted the Nectar of Immortality and squabbled over it to the extent that Vishnu, the creator and preserver, decided to settle the question of immortality once and for all. He disguised himself as a maiden and carried a jug of nectar. He passed the jug to the gods for a sip but, when he passed a demon, he flirted with them so as to distract them. By mistake, however, he gave the jug to the demon Rahu, who took a sip even though he was warned by the moon. Rahu is angry with the moon for betraying him and punishes it by giving it an eclipse once a year.

4

The Girl Who Had Seven Brothers

Seven brothers live with their seven wives and their sister, who they love dearly. When the girl celebrates her sixteenth birthday, the brothers know they have to arrange a marriage for her and reluctantly do so. She marries the handsome son of a rich landowner who lives two hundred miles away. They miss her and invite her and her husband to celebrate Karvachauth and, when she arrives, they notice how unwell she looks. She tells them she is fasting and, over the days, her health deteriorates but she refuses to eat until she sees the moon. They decide to play a trick on her so that she thinks she sees the moon and will eat and she falls for it. Her husband dies and she is angry with her brothers. She takes him to the forest and sits with his body for twelve months until the next Karvachauth celebration. The goddesses come and one by one they refuse to bring him back to life until the ninth goddess comes along and she begs at her feet relentlessly. She then restores life to her husband as long as she promises to fast from sunrise to sunset every Karvachauth.

Lakshmi and the Clever Washerwoman

The queen is spoiled by the king and, one year, she begs the king to get her a seven string necklace of pearls. He sends his men off to find the pearls and the queen is happy with her gift. However, disaster strikes when she goes to the river to bathe and a crow swoops down and steals her necklace. The king sets up a reward for the safe return of the necklace and, when it lands on a poor washerwoman's doorstep, she goes to the king. The washerwoman, who lives unhappily with a companion called Poverty, tells the king she does not want the reward. Instead she asks him to pass a law that says on Divali no one, apart from her, is allowed lights. The king agrees and so Lakshmi finds the one house with lights and asks to be let in. The washerwoman says she may enter if she promises to stay for seven generations and Poverty, who will not be in the same place as Lakshmi, agrees to leave for seven generations. The washerwoman is then blessed with wealth and prosperity.

The Wicked King and his Good Son

King Hiranya Kashyap believes himself to be immortal after a sage tells him he cannot be killed by man or beast or weapons during the day or night, underwater, inside a house or outside it. His sister Holika believes she cannot be burnt by fire. One day, Hiranya's wife has a son called Prahlad but, because he thinks he is immortal, he does not need an heir. His son, however, doesn't think he is god and when, at the age of five, he tells him this, his father sends him to be thrown off a cliff. Prahlad falls but is caught and survives. When the king hears what has happened, he orders Holika to sit with him in a fire, where she will be protected but he will burn to death. Holika softens and asks God to take her and to save the child and, when Hiranya hears of this, he ties Prahlad to a pillar and says he will kill him.

God appears out of the pillar in the form of half man and half lion, lifts the king and carries him to the threshold of the palace, where he kills him. Prahlad is crowned king.

The Mango Tree

A man lives with his wife and sister. His wife tends to the chores all day while his sister spends her day tending to her mango tree. The wife gets fed up and persuades her husband to marry his sister off. On her wedding day, just as she is about to leave the house, the sister asks the wife to care for the mango tree, but she decides to neglect it instead. Her husband becomes ill and grows weaker and the sister comes to visit. She sees that her mango tree is dying and tends to it, bringing it back to health. As this happens, her brother's health improves and she explains to his wife that her brother and the tree share the same soul.

The Faithful Sister

A shy girl longs for a baby brother to play with and, when she is fifteen, she gets her wish. She cares for him and loves him dearly until the day she has to leave home and marry. When the boy turns fifteen, he goes to his sister and asks her to the wedding. She promises she will, says she will follow him in a few days' time and sends him home with sweets for the journey. When he leaves, she realises the sweets have been poisoned and chases after her brother. She catches up with him, buries the food and goes with him to her parents' house. On the way, she meets a sage who tells her he will die, but that she can save him by pretending to be mad until his bride has been in the house for one day. She starts cursing him and carries on during the wedding celebrations. On his wedding day, she prods his crown with a needle and a dead viper comes out of it. She then demands to ride his horse and, as she mounts the gateway where they are standing, collapses and she is slightly injured. She finally demands the bridal bed and the family notice a scorpion in it. Once the bride has been in the house for a day, she explains what has happened and is given gifts.

The Old Man and the Magic Bowl

An old man loses his home due to illness and, during the Nine Days' Festival, he is told to go to Parvati's temple for help. Parvati gives him a bowl, tells him to wash it out and wish for whatever food he desires and it will appear. The bowl is so successful that he and his wife decide to invite the king for a meal. The king arrives and, when he realises what has happened, his prime minister asks for the bowl on behalf of the king. The old man starves again and, the following year, goes back and explains to Parvati what has happened. She gives him a rod and tells him to invite the king to dinner again. The rod starts hitting everyone and the king is told that it is because he has the bowl. The bowl is returned.

4

The King Without an Heir

One day, when King Rudra goes out, he is greeted by a washerman who looks him in the eye and spits. After this happens several times, the king stops to ask him why he does it. The man tells him he is unlucky because he doesn't have an heir and he spits to cancel out the bad luck. He tells his wife and she says that he should marry her sister and try for an heir with her. Again he has no luck and she advises him to marry her next sister. After the king has married all seven sisters and not produced an heir, he locks his wives in an attic. The queens decide they have to lie. They pretend that one of the sisters is pregnant and they are released from the attic to look after her. They fake the birth of a son and say the king cannot see him yet because he is delicate and that they have to go to Parvati's temple to pray for his health. Once there, they pray for a son and Parvati grants their wish. The queens then fight over who is to be the mother, but Parvati decides this too. The king is delighted when he sees his heir.

The Girl in the Forest

An orphaned girl lives in the forest and has to rely on charity to survive. One day, the king notices her, falls in love with her and marries her. After they are married, the king asks her what she is eating for breakfast and she lies and tells him it is pearls that her parents have sent when it is actually millet and barley. He asks to meet her family and she prays to Parvati for help. Parvati arranges for her to have a family that live in a palace, but that the wish will only be granted for three hours. The next day, the king realises he has left something behind and asks a servant to fetch it for him. The servant comes back with his belongings, but says he could not find the palace. The queen tells the king the truth and he says it does not matter.

How Ganesh got his Elephant Head

Parvati is married to Shiva but, because he is away for long periods of time, she gets lonely and decides to make a baby out of clay and breathe life into it. She calls him Ganesh and loves him dearly. One day, she goes to bathe and asks Ganesh to guard her so that no one interrupts her. Shiva returns home and demands to be let in, but Ganesh refuses so he cuts his head off. Parvati is angry with Shiva and explains that he is their son. She makes him go into the forest and bring the head of the first living thing he sees. He returns with an elephant head and attaches it to Ganesh.

Guided Reading – *Seasons of Splendour*

Reading objectives
- To analyse the features of a good opening and compare a number of story openings.
- To compare the structure of different stories, to discover how they differ in pace, build up, sequence, complication and resolution.
- To investigate how characters are presented, referring to the text: through dialogue, action and description; how the reader responds to them (as victims, heroes, etc); through examining their relationships with other characters.
- To consider how texts can be rooted in the writer's experience, e.g. friendship, holidays.

Session One

Introducing the text
Ask the children to read the introduction at the start of the book in preparation for the guided reading session. Talk to them about how, when the author was a child, the tradition of oral storytelling was the main way in which stories were passed down from generation to generation. Then ask them to think about why the author may have now decided to write these stories down.

Also talk to the children about how these books are short stories and how this means that we do not have to read them in the order presented to us – we can dip into them and select specific stories that we may wish to read. Explain that these stories in particular are seasonal and we may want to read a story to coincide with a particular festival or time of year, just as would have happened in the author's storytelling sessions at home.

Strategy check
Talk to the children about the way in which the book is structured. Show them that, before every section of stories, the author explains the background to any gods, festivals or feasts that the reader may need to know about or find interesting before they read those particular stories.

Independent reading
Explain to the children that you want them to read the first five pages of "Lakshmi and the Clever Washerwoman" up to "…well clothed for the rest of your days." and to think about the story structure the author uses to introduce and develop the story.

4

Return to the text
Discuss the following:
- How does the author start the story?
- Who are the main characters in the story?
- What is the major incident that happens?
- Describe the two characters of the washerwoman and Poverty. Use words from the text to help you.
- How do you think the washerwoman felt when she found the necklace?
- Do you think the washerwoman is going to accept the reward? Why do you think that?

Follow-up activity one
Ask the children to read to the end of the story and to write about what they would do if they were the washerwoman.

Follow-up activity two
Ask the children to read the "A SPECIAL BIRTHDAY" stories up the end of "The Serpent King". Ask them to write about how they think Krishna will kill King Kans.

Session Two

Response to the text
Discuss the following:

Lakshmi and the Clever Washerwoman
- Why did the washerwoman decide not to accept the reward?
- How did she get Poverty to leave?
- Do you think she wanted Poverty to leave? Why do you think that? Use words from the text to help you answer the question.
- What would you have done if you were the washerwoman? Why?

The Birth of Krishna
- How does the author start the story?
- Why do you think she starts it this way?
- Describe the character of King Kans?
- Why is his father in prison?
- Why does he put Devaki and Vasudev in prison?
- Why does he kill their babies?
- How do you think it is that Vasudev is able to leave the prison? Why is Krishna not killed?

4

Krishna and the Demon Nurse
- How do you think Kans feels when he hears that Krishna is alive? Why do you think that?
- Why does he hire Pootana?
- How does Pootana manage to trick Krishna's foster mother?
- Does Pootana succeed? Why not?

The Serpent King
- What happens in this story? Use words from the text to help you answer the question.
- How old is Krishna at this part of the story?
- What does it tell us about Krishna's personality?

Strategy check

Talk to the children about how the characters are presented and how we are made aware of whether they are good or evil. Ask them to think about some of the characters that we do not get to meet, but are aware of, for example Kans' father and Krishna's foster mother. Ask the children to think about whether they are victims or heroes and why.

Independent reading

Ask the children to read the first four pages of "How Krishna Killed the Wicked King Kans" up to 'Poor Krishna did not stand a chance.' Explain to them that you want them to think about the way the pace in the story is now being built up as the story heads towards its resolution. Ask them also to note down the type of language the author uses to portray Kans.

Return to the text

Discuss the following:
- Why does Kans decide to throw a party?
- How do you think he feels when he hears he has a nephew?
- How is Krishna described by Kans' informer?
- What does Kans decide to do?
- Do you think the author is right when she says Krishna doesn't stand a chance? Why do you think that?
- What language does the author use when discussing Kans? Why do you think she does this?
- What do you think will happen next?

Follow-up activity three

Ask the children to read to the end of the story and to make a mind map of Krishna.

Follow-up activity four

Ask the children to read "The Faithful Sister" and to then write their own story with the same title. Remind them to use a similar storytelling structure to the author.

4 Seasons of Splendour (1)

Name .... Date...........

What would you have done if you were the washerwoman?

Year 5 Enjoy Guided Reading © Badger Publishing Ltd.

4 **Seasons of Splendour (2)**

Name .... Date...........

The Slaying of King Kans

How do you think Krishna will kill King Kans?

4 Seasons of Splendour (3)

Name .... Date...........

Krishna

Make a mind map of Krishna.

Krishna

Year 5 Enjoy Guided Reading © Badger Publishing Ltd.

4 Seasons of Splendour (4)

Name .... Date............

The Faithful Sister

Make up you own story called 'The Faithful Sister'. Don't forget to use a similar storytelling structure to the author.

5 How the Whale Became and other stories
by Ted Hughes

Chapter Synopsis

Chapter 1 – Why the Owl Behaves as it does

One day, Owl realises that he is the only bird that can see at night. He is fed up with eating mice and rats, and would rather eat birds, so he decides to trick the birds into thinking that there is a better place to live. He tells them if he takes them there they will have to beware of the night, as the dark will kill them. The birds agree and, when they get there, they shut their eyes to the dark as the owl instructs them. What the birds don't realise is that the owl is tricking them and it is actually daytime but, while they are asleep, he eats a few of them – because their eyes are shut, the others don't notice. Finally, the birds have enough of scrabbling about in the dark searching for food and decide to die together in an act of bravery by keeping their eyes open when Owl tells them to shut them. They open their eyes, ready to die, but instead of seeing the dark they see the sunrise. They start singing and realise the trick that Owl has been playing on them. Owl hides from the birds by burying himself in a tree trunk and will now only dare come out when the birds are asleep. He is also back to a diet of mice and rats.

Chapter 2 – How the Whale Became

God sees a black seed in his garden. It is initially very small but soon starts to grow until it develops an eye and then a mouth. He tells God he's a Whale-Wort and God asks the other animals what he should do because he has grown so big that he has started to knock his house down. Mouse tells him to throw him into the sea, but he doesn't want to go. God tells him he can come back when he is smaller and makes a hole in his head. He explains that, if he blows out through the hole, he will get smaller. The Whale-Wort does as God tells him and he does get smaller, but then becomes so tired that he sinks to the bottom of the sea and falls asleep. When he wakes up, the Whale-Wort finds that he is bigger again and so floats back up to the surface to shrink. He soon realises that he will never make it back to God's garden and remains in the sea where the creatures call him whale.

Chapter 3 – How the Fox Came to be where it is

Dog and Fox are rivals for the job of guarding Man's farm. Man says they can decide between them which one of them will get the job. Fox has a secret plan and suggests that they ask the hens to decide. Dog agrees and Fox then tricks the rabbit by saying he can get her some cabbages. He leads her to the henhouse instead, eats the hens and then tells everyone that the rabbit ate them. Fox gets the job, but also gets a taste for the hens. One day, Dog sees Fox with some feathers around its mouth and remarks on it. Fox hatches a plan and starts by telling the farmer that Dog is killing the hens. He tells Dog to meet him in the henhouse, traps him in there and calls the farmer, but while he is waiting for him, can't help gloating. The farmer hears him so he runs away and Dog gets the job.

Chapter 4 – How the Polar Bear Became

The animals regularly hold beauty contests and it is always Polar Bear who wins. The other animals start to admire her and she beings to get vain to the extent that she refuses to go out when it rains in case she gets dirty. She decides that she wants to go somewhere cleaner to live. One day, Peregrine Falcon, who is jealous of Polar Bear always winning the contests, tells her he knows of a place made of white powder and where the rocks are mirrors. He hires a whale to take her and she lives happily with the seals there. Peregrine Falcon thinks he can now win the beauty contests but Mouse beats him to first prize.

Chapter 5 – How the Hyena Became

Hyena wants to be like Leopard, but he spends so much time copying Leopard that he never learns to kill his own food and has to eat Leopard's leftovers. He loves boasting to the other animals how similar he is to Leopard, but they tell him he is just a wild dog. One day, he wakes up and finds he has spots. He decides to go and scare the other wild dogs, who don't recognise him. When they realise who he is, they get angry with him, stop trusting him and move away when they see him. The truth dawns on him that he will never be a leopard and so he goes back to being a wild dog. He soon realises that he is unable to kill his own food and has to start following Leopard around and eating his leftovers.

Chapter 6 – How the Tortoise Became

When God makes the animals, he crafts them out of clay first and then, after they are baked in the oven, breathes life into them and gives them a skin. One day, God decides to make Tortoise, originally known as Torto. It is a hot day and God makes the mistake of breathing life into him before he is completely cool. Torto runs to the nearest stream to cool down and refuses when God tries to put his skin on. The other animals are horrified by his lack of skin and even more angry when he starts winning all the running competitions. Torto knows this is because he is so light and continues to refuse to have a skin until the other animals start to ignore him. He decides to ask God for a skin he can take on and off. It looks strange but he still keeps winning the races because he can take his skin off whenever he needs to. One day, after he has left his skin on for a few weeks and tries to take it off for a race, he finds it has got stuck. Much to his embarrassment, he finds he can't move very fast and loses the race. The other animals mock him, calling, "Who is the slowest…?" to which the others reply "Torto is!", which is how he got his name.

5

Chapter 7 – How the Bee Became
A demon with only one eye lives in the middle of the earth. His eye is made of fire, which he feeds with precious gems and metals that he mines. One day, he goes into the light and sees the animals that God has created and decides he wants to make one too. He steals some of God's clay but realises he needs water. He cries, but the mixture of his tears and the clay makes the clay disappear. He tries again with some of his ground up metals and his tears. This time he is successful and he makes a little creature that he bakes in the fire in his eye. He then tricks God into breathing life into it and they are amazed at its beauty. But his creature is sad because he has the demon's tears in his veins and the demon knows he has to cheer him up, so he gives him flowers to make him happy. The scent is so beautiful, the bee buzzes from flower to flower and, when the sweetness starts to ooze out of him, he makes a hive to store it all.

Chapter 8 – How the Cat Became
Most of the creatures are able to busy themselves during the day and sleep at night, but Cat annoys all the others by tuning his violin at night and then becomes so tired that he spends the day lazing about. The other animals get cross with him and worry that their children will copy his bad habits. They wake him up and tell him to get a job. Cat runs off and goes to Man's farm to see if he can get work there. Man says he would make a good rat and mouse catcher and, in exchange, will give him milk and meat and a place by the fireside. Cat is in his element, working by night and sleeping by day, and he also manages to fit in some violin playing. Mrs Man loves him too and all the other farmers decide to hire cats as well. So to this day, cats spend their evenings catching rats and mice and sleeping by day.

Chapter 9 – How the Donkey Became
Donkey, who is good at copying the other animals and finds it hard to settle to one thing, is unsure as to how he can earn a living. He is so good at imitating the other animals that he doesn't learn to get his own food and has to beg the other animals for food, but they soon get tired of him. One day, he meets a man who is tired of drawing water from his well and Donkey decides to help him. In exchange for work, the man gives him a barn to live in and Donkey is happy with the arrangement as it means that he can still practise being like the other animals. One day, Lion asks him to leap and roar, but Donkey doesn't do it well. After his disappointment wears off, he decides to stop trying to be like the other animals and to be himself.

Chapter 10 – How the Hare Became
Hare is so vain that one of the other animals, Gazelle, gets tired of him and decides to trick him. He tells him he is handsome and that the moon has been talking about him and wants to marry him. He tells Hare where to meet her.

5

He goes to see her but she is far away and he thinks he has the wrong hill. He chases after her, never quite catching her, but tries to hear what she is saying about him. He hears nothing and tells the other animals, who all smile, knowing he has fallen for their trick. Hare stares constantly at the moon so that his face takes on a startled look and he becomes a fast runner. His ears also grow through straining to hear what the moon is saying and that is how he has developed into the creature we know today.

Chapter 11 – How the Elephant Became

Bombo the Elephant doesn't know what to become. He thinks he's slow and stupid and knows he has to do something but is not sure what. He tries out some tricks but the others just laugh at him and so he moves to an island, where he lives with some birds and beetles. One day, there is a forest fire and the animals start to panic. Bombo goes to rescue the animals, they climb on his back and he takes them to the safety of his island but, when he gets there, the fire reaches the island. He uses his tusks to dig up the trees and clears the land, so the fire doesn't spread, and he saves everyone. The animals see Bombo as their hero and want to crown him king, but he is shy and hides away.

Guided Reading – *How the Whale Became and other stories*

Reading objectives

- To develop an active attitude towards reading: seeking answers, anticipating events, empathising with characters and imagining events that are described.
- To change point of view, e.g. tell incident or describe a situation from the point of view of another character or perspective.

Session One

Introducing the text

Ask the children to read the introduction so that they gain an understanding of the premise for the book. Discuss with them what other ways the animals could evolve and pool the ideas together so that the children can use them in their own story writing.

5

Strategy check

Remind the children that the book is set in the past and that, although we know the characteristics that these animals possess now, for example we know that foxes are reputed to be sly, at the time these characteristics weren't known and the stories tell us how they came about. Also talk to the children about how these books are short stories and how this means that we do not have to read them in the order presented to us – we can dip into them and select specific stories that we may wish to read.

Independent reading

Explain to the children that the first story we are going to select is "How the Fox Became" and ask them to read the first five pages up to "...feather in the corner of your mouth." Ask them to think about how Fox is earning his reputation of being sly.

Return to the text

Discuss the following:
- Why do Foursquare and Slylooking want to work for Man?
- Why do you think the author gave the two animals these names?
- Do you think that Man knows of Fox's reputation? Why do you think that?
- Why does Rabbit believe Slylooking?
- Why does Foursquare think Rabbit ate the hens?
- What is Slylooking's weakness?
- Why does Foursquare suspect Slylooking?
- What do you think Slylooking will do now? Why do you think that?

Follow-up activity one

Ask the children to read the end of the story and to map it out in sequence.

Follow-up activity two

Explain to the children that you want them to rewrite the story from Foursquare's perspective. Remind them that Foursquare will not know about Slylooking's reputation and so will not think he has got the job unfairly.

Session Two

Response to the text
Discuss the following:
- Why does Foursquare's comment make Slylooking nervous?
- Why does Man agree with Slylooking when he says that it could all be Foursquare's fault?
- How does he try to trick Foursquare?
- Why does his trick work to start with?
- What is it that Slylooking does that gives the game away?
- How is Slylooking punished?
- How is Foursquare rewarded?
- How does Fox get his name?

Strategy check
Remind the children to note punctuation when reading and how this and using expression can enhance their reading.

Independent reading
Ask the children to read the first three pages of "How the Whale Became" up to "What are we going to do with it?" Ask the children to think about how the Whale-Wort must be feeling about the size he is growing to.

Return to the text
Discuss the following:
- Where do you think the Whale-Wort came from?
- How does God feel about it growing bigger and bigger in his garden?
- Why is God worried about its size?
- How do you think the Whale-Wort must feel about his size? Why do you think that?
- Where do you think the Whale-Wort wants to live? Why do you think that?
- What do you think God should do with the Whale-Wort? Why?

Follow-up activity three
Ask the children to read to the end of the story and to think about another sea creature, for example a jellyfish or a shark. Ask them to map out the story of how this sea creature became.

Follow-up activity four
Ask the children to read the rest of the stories and to write about which is their favourite.

5 How the Whale Became and other stories (1)

Name .... Date............

Slylooking's Story

Ask the children to read the end of "How the Fox Became" and to map out the story in sequence.

5 How the Whale Became and other stories (2)

Name .... Date............

Foursquare's Story

Rewrite "How the Fox Became" from Foursquare's perspective. Remember that Foursquare will not know about Slylooking's reputation and so will not think he has got the job unfairly.

Year 5 Enjoy Guided Reading © Badger Publishing Ltd.

5   How the Whale Became and other stories (3)

Name .... Date............

My Sea Creature and How it Became

Map out the story of how another sea creature, such as a jelly fish or a shark, became.

Year 5 Enjoy Guided Reading © Badger Publishing Ltd.

5 How the Whale Became and other stories (4)

Name .... Date............

My Favourite Story

Which is your favourite story and why? Use evidence from the text to support your ideas.

Year 5 Enjoy Guided Reading © Badger Publishing Ltd.

6 The Snow Goose and other stories
by Paul Gallico

Story Synopsis – "The Snow Goose"

Philip Rhayader has withdrawn from the world because of his physical appearance. He lives in an abandoned lighthouse, where he spends his time painting and caring for birds. One day, a local twelve year old girl called Fritha brings him a wounded bird and asks him to heal it. He tells her it is a snow goose from Canada and that it was probably heading south when it got caught in a storm, decided to rest and was shot by a hunter. Just as she is about to leave, Philip invites her back to check on her bird and she becomes a regular visitor until it is time again for it to go to its breeding ground. Fritha stops visiting and Philip becomes lonely again. The goose comes back the next year and he leaves word for her in the village, so she starts to visit again. One year, the snow goose doesn't return and Philip is heartbroken but, the next year, when it comes it decides to stay. Fritha, who has now grown into a woman, says goodbye to Philip and tells him he won't be lonely now he has the bird for company but, three weeks later, she decides to visit again and sees Philip packing. He tells her he is going to help rescue the British Army from the Dunkirk beaches and asks her to look after the bird sanctuary he has built up. The snow goose follows him.

The story is now retold by eye witnesses who were rescued by Philip. We know it is him because the snow goose circles above the boat at all times. He helps to clear the beach and, when all the soldiers are rescued, he waves goodbye and sets off home. Other eye witnesses talk of how the snow goose took on an air of folklore that said if you saw the snow goose you would be saved. They say that, once the beach was cleared, they saw a derelict small boat with a bird perched on the side. As they got closer, they saw the body of a man lying face down in the boat. He had been shot. Their attention was distracted and, when they looked again, the boat had sunk.

Back at the lighthouse, Fritha waits for Philip but, when she sees the snow goose flying back, her worst fears are confirmed. The bird circles above, saying goodbye, and then leaves. Fritha realises it is Philip coming to say goodbye to her and she tells him she loves him. Fritha continues to look after the birds until, one day, the lighthouse is blown up by a German plane thinking it is still operative.

6

Guided Reading – *The Snow Goose and other stories*

Reading objectives
- To investigate how characters are presented, referring to the text: through dialogue, action and description; how the reader responds to them (as victims, heroes); through examining their relationships with other characters.
- To consider how texts can be rooted in the writer's experience, e.g. historical events and places, experiences of wartime, friendship, holidays.
- To change a point of view, e.g. tell incident or describe a situation from the point of view of another character or perspective.

Session One

Introducing the text
Show the children the book and ask them to find out when the story was first written. Explain to them that it is a reprint and that it was first printed in 1941. Ask the children what was happening in the world at that time and, considering the fact that the story focuses on one particular incident in the Second World War, whether the author may have been writing from an experienced viewpoint. Explore the idea with the children that, although he may not have been part of what was happening at Dunkirk, he may know about it through speaking to people who were there or reading about it in the newspapers.

Strategy check
Explain to the children that the first section of the book is very descriptive and that they may find it useful to make notes as they go along.

Independent reading
Ask the children to read up to 'And this made Philip happy.' (page 2) and to think about how the story and the main character are introduced to us and how we respond to Philip Rhayadar as a character.

Return to the text
Discuss the following:
- Where is the story set?
- Describe the setting, using words from the text to help you.
- Where does Philip live?
- Describe his physical appearance, using words from the text to help you.
- What was Philip like as a person? How do you know?
- Who has been telling us the story so far?

65

6

Follow-up activity one
Ask the children to write a character passport of Philip.

Follow-up activity two
Explain to the children that you want them to read the next four sections up to '...back to the empty lighthouse.' (page 15) and to make notes on how Philip's life changes when the snow goose returns.

Session Two

Response to the text
Discuss the following:
- Describe Philip.
- Why does he withdraw from the world?
- If he knows that men like him, why is he uncomfortable about letting them get close?
- How does he spend his days?
- Is Philip a good painter? How do you know?
- How does Fritha feel about approaching the lighthouse?
- What has happened to the Snow Goose?
- How does Philip's life change when the snow goose comes back?
- Who do you think Philip misses most when the snow goose is away? Why do you think that?
- Why does Fritha say goodbye when the snow goose decides to stay?
- Where does Philip go?
- What do you think will happen to him?

Strategy check
Explain to the children that the next part of the story is told by eye witnesses and so the tone changes. Explain to them that the author uses colloquial language and that it may help them if they read aloud.

Independent reading
Ask the children to read up to '"He did," said Jock.' (page 19) While they read, ask them to think about the effect this has on the story and why the author has decided to do it.

6

Return to the text

Discuss the following:
- Who tells the next part of the story?
- How do they describe the snow goose?
- Describe the scene that awaits Philip when he arrives.
- How do they describe Philip's boat?
- How do we know they are describing Philip?
- Was Philip a hero? How do you know?

Follow-up activity three

Ask the children to read to the end of the story and to imagine they are the author. Ask them to rewrite the Dunkirk part of the story.

Follow-up activity four

Explain to the children that you want them to read the other short stories and to choose their favourite, and to then sequence the events of the story in the order they happen.

6 The Snow Goose and other stories (1)

Name .... Date............

PHILIP RHAYADER

Make a character passport of Philip:

Name ....

Appearance ....
....
....
....
....

Personality ....
....
....
....

Other important information ....
....
....
....
....

Year 5 Enjoy Guided Reading © Badger Publishing Ltd.

6 The Snow Goose and other stories (2)

Name . . . . Date. . . . .

The Snow Goose Returns

Make notes on how Philip's life changes when the snow goose returns.

6 The Snow Goose and other stories (3)

Name .... Date ....

Dunkirk

Imagine you are the author. Rewrite the Dunkirk part of the story from the narrator's perspective.

Year 5 Enjoy Guided Reading © Badger Publishing Ltd.

6 The Snow Goose and other stories (4)

Name .... Date............

Mapping the Story

Choose one of the other stories and sequence the events of the story in the order they happen.

Badger Publishing Limited
15 Wedgwood Gate
Pin Green Industrial Estate
Stevenage, Hertfordshire SG1 4SU
Telephone: 01438 356907
Fax: 01438 747015
www.badger-publishing.co.uk
enquiries@badger-publishing.co.uk

Enjoy Guided Reading!
Year 5 Teacher Book with Copymasters

First published 2005
ISBN 1 84424 658 2

Text © Sarah St John 2005
Complete work © Badger Publishing Limited 2005

The right of Sarah St John to be identified as author of this Work has been asserted by her in accordance with the Copyright, Designs and Patents Act 1988.

You may copy this book freely for use in your school.
The pages in this book are copyright, but copies may be made without fees or prior permission provided that these copies are used only by the institution which purchased the book. For copying in any other circumstances, prior written consent must be obtained from the publisher.

Publisher: David Jamieson
Editor: Paul Martin
Designer: Adam Wilmott

Printed in the UK

Enjoy Guided Reading!

Guided Reading guidance on 40 popular reading books and novels

NEW

The Teacher Books:

Level 2A Teacher Book with Copymasters	ISBN 1 84424 654 X
Level 2A+ – 3 Teacher Book with Copymasters	ISBN 1 84424 655 8
Year 3 Teacher Book with Copymasters	ISBN 1 84424 656 6
Year 4 Teacher Book with Copymasters	ISBN 1 84424 657 4
Year 5 Teacher Book with Copymasters	ISBN 1 84424 658 2
Year 6 Teacher Book with Copymasters	ISBN 1 84424 659 0

KS2 covers the following novels, available in packs of 6 from Badger Publishing:

Year 3

George's Marvellous Medicine by Roald Dahl	ISBN 1 84424 691 4
The Hodgeheg by Dick King-Smith	ISBN 1 84424 692 2
The Julian Stories by Ann Cameron	ISBN 1 84424 693 0
The True Story of the 3 Little Pigs by Jon Scieszka & Lane Smith	ISBN 1 84424 694 9
The Three Little Wolves and the Big Bad Pig by Eugene Triviazas & Helen Oxenbury	ISBN 1 84424 695 7
The Otter Who Wanted to Know by Jill Tomlinson	ISBN 1 84424 696 5

Year 4

James and the Giant Peach by Roald Dahl	ISBN 1 84424 697 3
The Lion, the Witch and the Wardrobe by C.S. Lewis	ISBN 1 84424 698 1
The Worst Witch by Jill Murphy	ISBN 1 84424 699 X
It's Too Frightening for Me by Shirley Hughes	ISBN 1 84424 700 7
Dinosaurs and all that Rubbish by Michael Foreman	ISBN 1 84424 701 5
The Enchanted Horse by Magdalen Nabb	ISBN 1 84424 702 3

Year 5

Charlotte's Web by E.B. White	ISBN 1 84424 703 1
Goodnight Mister Tom by Michelle Magorian	ISBN 1 84424 704 X
The Illustrated Mum by Jacqueline Wilson	ISBN 1 84424 705 8
Seasons of Splendour by Madhur Jaffrey	ISBN 1 84424 706 6
How the Whale Became and other stories by Ted Hughes	ISBN 1 84424 707 4
The Snow Goose and other stories by Paul Gallico	ISBN 1 84424 708 2

Year 6

Bad Girls by Jacqueline Wilson	ISBN 1 84424 709 0
The Indian in the Cupboard by Lynne Reid Banks	ISBN 1 84424 710 4
The Blurred Man by Anthony Horowitz	ISBN 1 84424 711 2
Tales from India retold by J.E.B. Gray	ISBN 1 84424 712 0
The Railway Children by E. Nesbit	ISBN 1 84424 713 9
The Secret Garden by Frances Hodgson-Burnett	ISBN 1 84424 714 7

Badger Key Stage 2 Guided Reading

Guided Reading guidance on 24 popular reading books and novels

The Teacher Books:

Year 3 Teacher Book with Copymasters	ISBN 1 84424 404 0
Year 4 Teacher Book with Copymasters	ISBN 1 84424 405 9
Year 5 Teacher Book with Copymasters	ISBN 1 84424 406 7
Year 6 Teacher Book with Copymasters	ISBN 1 84424 407 5

Covering the following novels, available in packs of 6 from Badger Publishing:

Year 3

Dear Greenpeace by Simon Jones	ISBN 1 84424 441 5
Have You Seen Who's Just Moved in Next Door to Us? by Colin McNaughton	ISBN 1 84424 442 3
The Magic Finger by Roald Dahl	ISBN 1 84424 443 1
The Diary of a Killer Cat by Anne Fine	ISBN 1 84424 444 X
Dragon Ride by Helen Cresswell	ISBN 1 84424 445 8
Grandpa Chatterji by Jamila Gavin	ISBN 1 84424 446 6

Year 4

The Owl Tree by Jenny Nimo	ISBN 1 84424 447 4
The Iron Man by Ted Hughes	ISBN 1 84424 448 2
Bill's New Frock by Anne Fine	ISBN 1 84424 449 0
Conker by Michael Morpurgo	ISBN 1 84424 450 4
Freckle Juice by Judy Blume	ISBN 1 84424 451 2
Blessu / Dumpling by Dick King-Smith	ISBN 1 84424 514 4 / 515 2

Year 5

Stig of the Dump by Clive King	ISBN 1 84424 453 9
Street Child by Berlie Doherty	ISBN 1 84424 454 7
Butterfly Lion by Michael Morpurgo	ISBN 1 84424 455 5
The Mousehole Cat by Antonia Barber	ISBN 1 84424 456 3
The Stinky Cheese Man by Jan Scieszka	ISBN 1 84424 457 1
Aquila by Andrew Norris	ISBN 1 84424 458 X

Year 6

Carrie's War by Nina Bawden	ISBN 1 84424 459 8
Tom's Midnight Garden by Phillippa Pearce	ISBN 1 84424 460 1
The Wreck of the Zanzibar by Michael Morpurgo	ISBN 1 84424 461 X
Over Sea, Under Stone by Susan Cooper	ISBN 1 84424 462 8
The Summerhouse by Alison Prince	ISBN 1 84424 463 6
The Lottie Project by Jacqueline Wilson	ISBN 1 84424 464 4

For details of the full range of books and resources from

Badger Publishing

including

- Book Boxes for Early Years, Infants, Juniors and Special Needs
- Badger Guided Reading for KS2 and book packs
- Badger Nursery Rhymes - A3 cards and teacher book
- Full Flight, Dark Flight & Rex Jones for reluctant readers
- Brainwaves - Non-fiction to get your brain buzzing!
- First Facts - non-fiction for infants
- Teaching Writing and Writing Poetry - for Years 1-6
- Expert at... English and Speaking & Listening - Copymaster books
- Delbert's Worksheets and Practice Questions for the KS1-2 Maths SATs
- Badger Maths: Problem Solving Books 1-2
- Badger KS2 Revision Quizzes for English, Maths and Science
- Badger Test Revision Guides for English, Maths and Science
- SATs Practice Papers for English, Maths and Science
- Badger RE - complete course for the primary school
- Badger Geography - complete course for the primary school
- Badger Science - complete course for the primary school
- Badger Comprehension - complete course for the primary school
- Badger ICT - complete course for the primary school
- Badger Citizenship & PSHE - complete course for the primary school
- Basic Background Knowledge - History, Geography
- Badger History for KS1 - big books and teacher books
- Badger Assembly Stories - for KS1-2

CD versions of many titles also now available.

See our full colour catalogue (available on request) or visit our website for more information:

www.badger-publishing.co.uk

Contact us at:

Badger Publishing Limited
15 Wedgwood Gate, Pin Green Industrial Estate,
Stevenage, Hertfordshire SG1 4SU
Telephone: 01438 356907
Fax: 01438 747015
enquiries@badger-publishing.co.uk

Or visit our brand new showroom at the new premises.